'Round-the-World
FOLKTALE
Mini-Books

13 Easy-to-Make Books to
Promote Literacy and Cultural Awareness

by Maria Fleming

SCHOLASTIC
PROFESSIONAL BOOKS

New York • Toronto • London • Auckland • Sydney

Cover design by Vincent Ceci and Frank Maiocco
Cover photograph by Donnelly Marks
Interior illustration by Kate Flanagan, Janice Fried,
Michelle Hill, John Jones and Phillip Smith
Book design by Carmen Robert Sorvillo
Copyright © 1995 by Maria Fleming
Printed in USA

12 11 10 9 8 7 6 5 4 3 2   8 9/9
ISBN 0-590-49793-6

CONTENTS

Introduction

How to Use the Mini-Books

Resources

The Tales

Introduction

As any teacher who has worked with mini-books knows, there is something very appealing about little books that can fit into the palm of even the smallest hands. This book is a collection of illustrated, reproducible patterns and directions for creating small books that feature folktales from around the world. Each book is in a special format that offers children some element of surprise: flaps to lift, tabs to pull, pictures that pop up, and more.

The book-making activities and stories can be used with a range of grades and reading levels. Some patterns are more complicated than others, but all—with varying amounts of guidance—can be completed by young children. Inside, you'll find some new twists on some old favorites, such as *The Three Billygoats Gruff* and *The Teeny Tiny Woman*. You'll also find some stories from countries as diverse as Australia, Nigeria, and France that children are probably unacquainted with. Because all of these folktales have endured through the centuries, you'll find that they have a broad range of appeal and should capture the interest of both older and younger children.

We hope that the special formats for these stories will delight and engage students and, in the process, motivate and inspire them in your reading curriculurm.

How to Use the Mini-Books

While these books are designed to enrich your reading program, they can be used in a variety of ways. You may want to use them as a resource in your classroom publishing center, to provide models for students as they write and create their own books. Perhaps you teach a genre unit focusing on folktales, fairy tales, fables, or tall tales; you'll find a number of mini-books here to include in your unit. You may want to incoporate some selections into theme studies on plants, animals, weather, or other topics. And, of course, these books can also be used to enhance studies of cultures around the world.

Following are a few additional ideas:

• Because a country's folklore migrates with its people, different versions of the same story are told around the world. Children may be familiar with some of the tales in this book in other forms, with variations that reflect their country of origin. Invite

students to compare and contrast the tales, using charts or Venn diagrams.

• Children will be folding pieces of paper into equal parts and sequencing pages as they make the books. Use the book-making activities to teach and enforce math concepts involving fractions, shapes, patterns, and symmetry.

• Use the books as an opportunity for sharing and interacting among grade levels. Invite older students in to help younger students assemble the books. Or if your students are older, you may want to have them make extra copies of the books which they can then read to a younger class. Leave the books as a gift from your class to theirs.

• Make your own pop-up books. These books use just a few simple devices to create an element of surprise. Once children have mastered the devices, they'll want to employ them to make pop-up versions of their own favorite folktales. This is an excellent problem-solving activity since children will have to determine which devices lend themselves to which stories. Encourage students to use their imaginations to develop new devices as well.

• Make several copies of each book to set up a mini-book folktale library, which children can add to during the year as they create their own books.

• Make tape recordings of some of the folktales (complete with cues for turning the pages). Then supply your Listening Center with several mini-book copies of each tale and use the cassette and books for small group reading or independent reading.

• Send the pattern for one tale home with children. Children can make and read the story with a parent, guardian, or older sibling for an excellent at-home shared reading experience.

Some Helpful Hints for Making the Books:

Trouble-shooting Tips!

Make each mini-book yourself before beginning a book-making project with children to familiarize yourself with the directions and how the book works. Then read the directions and make the books with children, checking their steps as you go along. This way, you'll be better able to trouble-shoot if children encounter any problems. You may want to have parent volunteers on hand to help out as well. Directions for assembling the books vary for each tale, but some general rules apply.

• Remove each mini-book at perforations and copy on a double-sided copier. You will need to experiment in order to align the type on both sides of each mini-book page. If you do not have access to a double-sided copier, the copying process will obviously take more time. Be careful not to invert the pattern on the back of the page as you make your copies or the patterns and directions for the books will not work properly.

• Solid lines are cut lines. Dotted lines are fold lines.

• Many of the books have interior folds and flaps. The easiest way to cut open an interior flap is to have students fold the page loosely across the cut line, so that the fold is at a right angle to the line. Students should snip on the line, and then, if more cutting is necessary, open out the fold, and insert the scissors into the slit they've just snipped. They can then cut easily along the rest of the cut line.

• Since many of the books involve two or more pages, each one is identified by a letter (A, B, C, or D) at the top to help children easily find the page they should be working with. (These letters are also a clue as to whether the page should be positioned vertically or horizontally on the desk.)

• For fun, invite children to color the books.

• Opening the book flat at the middle and stapling through the center spine will produce a binding like that of this book you are holding. It's recommended for all except *Antonio's Lucky Day*.

Resources

Africa

The Adventures of Spider: West African Folk Tales by Joyce C. Arkhurt, Little, Brown, 1992.

Anansi, the Spider by Gerald McDermott, Henry Holt, 1987. (WEST AFRICA)

Beat the Story Drum, Pum-Pum by Ashley Bryan, Macmillan, 1980.

Bringing the Rain to Kapiti Plain retold by Verna Aardema, Dial, 1979. (NANDI/EAST AFRICA)

The Egyptian Cinderella by Shirley Climo, Crowell, 1989. (EGYPT)

How Many Spots Does a Leopard Have? by Julius Lester, Scholastic, 1989.

How the Guinea Fowl Got Her Spots: A Swahili Tale of Friendship retold by Barbara Knutson, Lerner/ Carolrhoda, 1990.

Lion and the Ostrich Chicks and Other African Tales retold by Ashley Bryan, Atheneum, 1986.

Mufaro's Beautiful Daughters by John Steptoe, Lothrop, 1987.

Travelling to Tondo retold by Verna Aardema, Knopf, 1991.

Why Mosquitoes Buzz in People's Ears retold by Verna Aardema, Dial, 1975.

Asia

The Bird Who Was an Elephant by Aleph Kamal, HarperCollins, 1990. (INDIA)

The Golden Serpent by Walter Dean Myers, Viking, 1980. (INDIA)

Liang and the Magic Paintbrush by Demi, Holt, Rinehart and Winston, 1980. (CHINA)

Lon Po Po: A Red Riding Hood Tale from China translated by Ed Young, Philomel, 1989.

The Magic Boat by Demi, Henry Holt, 1990. (CHINA)

The Monkey and the Crocodile by Paul Galdone, Clarion, 1979. (INDIA)

Nine-in-One, Grrr! Grrr! by Xiong Blia, Childrens Book Press, 1989. (HMONG)

Once There Was and Twice There Wasn't by Barbara K. Walker, Follett, 1968. (TURKEY)

The Seven Chinese Brothers by Margaret Mahy, Scholastic, 1990.

Australia

The Singing Snake by Stefan Czernecki and Timothy Rhodes, Hyperion, 1993.

What Made Tiddalik Laugh retold by Joanna Troughton, Peter Bedrick Books, 1977.

Europe

East of the Sun and West of the Moon by Mercer Mayer, Macmillan, 1987. (NORWAY)

The Hedgehog Boy by Jane Langton, HarperCollins, 1985. (LATVIA)

Jamie O'Rourke and the Big Potato by Tomie dePaola, Putnam, 1992. (IRELAND)

The Little Snowgirl by Carolyn Croll, Putnam, 1989. (RUSSIA)

The Shoemaker and the Elves by Jakob and Wilhelm Grimm/Ilse Plume, Harcourt Brace Jovanovich, 1991. (GERMANY)

Three Rolls and One Doughnut by Mirra Ginsburg, Dial, 1970. (RUSSIA)

Why the Sea Is Salt retold by Vivian French, Candlewich Press, 1993. (NORWAY)

The Legend of the Indian Paintbrush by Tomie de Paola, Putnam, 1987.

Song of Sedna adapted by Robert D. San Souci, Doubleday, 1981. (INUIT)

The Story of Jumping Mouse by John Steptoe, Lothrop, 1984. (NATIVE AMERICAN)

The Talking Eggs by Robert San Souci, Dial, 1989. (SOUTHERN UNITED STATES)

The Woman Who Outshone the Sun by Alejandro Cruz Martinez, Children's Book Press, 1991. (MEXICO)

North America

Borreguita and the Coyote by Verna Aardema, Knopf, 1991. (MEXICO)

The Boy Who Could Do Anything & Other Mexican Folk Tales retold by Anita Brenner, Linnet Books, 1992.

From Sea to Shining Sea: A Treasury of American Folklore compiled by Amy L. Cohn, Scholastic, 1993.

Keepers of the Animals: Native American Stories and Wildlife Activities for Children by Michael J. Caduto and Joseph Bruchac, Fulcrum, 1991.

Keepers of the Earth: Native American Stories and Environmental Activities for Children by Michael J. Caduto and Joseph Bruchac, Fulcrum, 1988.

Collections from Around the World

Best-Loved Folktales Around the World selected by Joanna Cole, Doubleday, 1982.

Favorite Fairy Tales Told Around the World selected by Virginia Haviland, Morrow, 1994.

Favorite Folktales from Around the World edited by Jane Yolen, Pantheon, 1986.

South and North, East and West: The Oxfam Book of Children's Stories edited by Michael Rosen, Candlewick Press, 1992.

World Folktales by Atelia Clarkson and Gilbert B. Cross, Scribner's, 1980.

Africa

WHY THE SUN AND MOON LIVE IN THE SKY

A pourquoi tale, this story from Nigeria explains how the sun and moon came to be in the sky. Children will construct a book with five simple folds.

Preparation:

Provide each child with a double-sided photocopy of page A. (One piece of paper, art and text on front and back.)

To Make the Mini-Book:

1. Place page A on the desk vertically.
2. Fold the top edge and bottom edge of the page toward the center by folding along the dotted lines. Crease sharply.
3. Fold the top and the bottom toward the center again by folding along the dotted lines. Crease sharply.
4. Fold the paper in half along the dotted line, folding the top down to meet the bottom so that the title of the book is face-up. Crease sharply.

Tips for Reading:

Unfold the top and bottom sections in reverse order to read the story. Be sure to unfold both the top and bottom of the page at the same time so that the illustrations correspond with the text. As children unfold the pages, they will watch the sun and moon rise higher and higher into the sky.

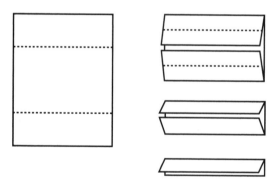

When it was completed, he asked the water to come and visit. When the water arrived, he called out to the sun and asked him whether it would be safe for him to enter.

"Yes, come in, my friend," the sun answered.

The water then began to flow in, accompanied by the fish and all the water animals. Very soon, the water had flooded the entire house, so the sun and moon had to perch themselves on top of the roof.

Many years ago the sun and the water were great friends, and both lived on the earth together. One evening, the sun invited the water to his home to meet his wife, the moon.

"If you wish me to visit, you must build a very large compound as my people are numerous and take up a lot of room," the moon told the sun. So the next day, the sun began building a huge compound in which to entertain his friend.

WHY THE SUN AND MOON LIVE IN THE SKY

A Folktale from Nigeria

The water again addressed the sun, "Do you want more of my people to come?" Not wanting to be rude, the foolish sun and moon both answered, "Yes." More of the water came rushing in, and very soon it overflowed the top of the roof. The sun and moon were forced to go up into the sky, where they have remained ever since.

THE OSTRICH AND THE CROCODILE

Children will construct a book with a sliding strip to read this "pourquoi" tale from Kenya that tells how the ostrich acquired its unusual neck.

Preparation:

Provide each child with a single-sided photocopy of panel B on this page and a double-sided photocopy of page A. Children will need tape and scissors to make the book.

To Make the Mini-Book:

1. Cut out panel B on the right-hand side of this page. Set aside.
2. Place page A on the desk horizontally.
3. Fold the page in half along the dotted line, folding the bottom of the page up to meet the top. The text and illustrations should now be face-up.
4. Open the fold of page A and place panel B inside so that the text and illustrations are face-up.
5. Tape along the top edges of the folded paper to hold panel B inside page A, as shown in the diagram.

(continued on back)

13

C

Then suddenly, "Ahhhh-CHOOO!" Crocodile sneezed. And as she did, Ostrich escaped, running from the river as fast as he could.

Ever since that day, Ostriches have had long necks. But they're careful to stay far, far away from clever crocodiles.

Panel B

(NOTE: When taping the edges closed, be careful not to tape down panel B. You should be able to slide panel B smoothly through folded page A.)

6. Pull panel B slightly out of the folded page, until both halves of dot C are aligned and the ostrich's body is aligned with its neck.

Tips for Reading:

Read the text on the front of the book first, then pull the right end of the sliding strip to watch Ostrich's neck grow longer and longer.

THE OSTRICH AND THE CROCODILE

A Folktale from Kenya

Long ago, Ostrich had a short neck, like all the other birds. One day, Ostrich was walking along when he met Crocodile.

"Oh, friend Ostrich, I have a terrible toothache. Will you help me by pulling the bad tooth?" Crocodile asked, opening her mouth wide.

Now Ostrich wasn't very smart, but he was kind. "I'll try," he said. He put his head deep inside Crocodile's mouth to hunt for the bad tooth.

Quick as a flash, sly Crocodile snapped shut her jaws, pleased that she had tricked Ostrich into becoming her lunch. But Ostrich didn't want to be Crocodile's lunch.

"Let me out!" Ostrich cried as he tried to pull his head free. Ostrich pulled and pulled, and as he pulled his neck stretched longer and longer.

Åsia

RUMORS

The Jatakas are a collection of more than 500 ancient tales from India. Written in the second and third century B.C., these fables are predominantly about the different incarnations of the Buddha, when he walked the earth in animal form. Children will make a simple accordian-book version of this Jataka tale, which they may enjoy comparing to the familiar story of "Henny Penny" who fears that the sky is falling.

Preparation:

Provide each child with a double-sided photocopy of page A. Children will need scissors and tape to make the book.

To Make the Mini-Book:

1. Place page A horizontally on the desk so that the letter A is at the top of the page.
2. Fold the right edge and the left edge of the page in toward the center, folding along the two vertical dotted lines. Crease well and unfold.
3. Flip the page over. Fold the page in half along the long vertical fold line. Crease well and unfold.
4. Flip the page back over to side A. Cut along the solid line to create two panels.
5. Lay the panels end to end so that the squares on each end meet, as shown in diagram. Tape together.
6. Flip the strip over and fold the center of the strip (where the two panels join) along the dotted line. Crease well.
7. Refold the pages back and forth along the creases to complete the accordian book.

Tips for Reading:

Hold the book so that the cover faces up. Unfold the first side of the accordian-strip slowly to read the beginning of the tale, then refold the pages, flip the book over, and unfold again to read the ending.

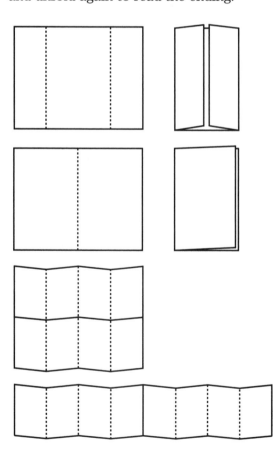

Rumors

A Jataka Tale from India

1

One day, a hare was sleeping beneath a tree when a big ripe fruit fell down with a loud THUD! that shook the ground.

2

The hare jumped up in surprise and started running. And as he ran, he shouted, "The earth is breaking apart! The earth is breaking apart!"

3

A deer saw the hare running. "What is the matter?" she asked. "The earth is breaking apart!" said the terrified hare. And the deer, too, began to run.

4

A rhinoceros saw the hare and the deer running. "What is the matter?" he asked. "The earth is breaking apart!" they said. And the rhino, too, began to run.

5

A tiger saw the hare, the deer, and the rhino running. "What is the matter?" she asked. "The earth is breaking apart!" they said. And the tiger, too, began to run.

6

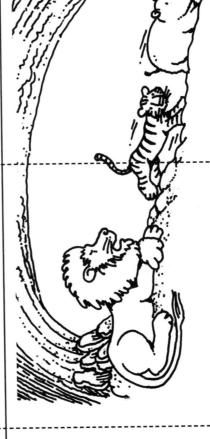

A lion sleeping in a nearby cave heard the animals thundering by. "What is the matter?" he asked.

7

"The earth is breaking apart!" said the animals, panting for breath.

8

"It was the hare," said the deer.

Then all of the animals looked at the hare.

13

"It's all true," he said. "I heard the terrible noise with my own ears and felt the earth tremble with my own feet." Then he took them to the spot where he had heard the noise.

14

Just as all the animals reached the tree, another big ripe fruit fell to the earth with a loud THUD!

15

The lion laughed and said to the hare, "The earth isn't breaking apart. You only heard this fruit hitting the ground.

Then the lion said to all the animals:

This advice,
I give to you-
Don't listen to rumors,
They are often untrue.

The End

16

But the earth seemed quite solid beneath the lion's feet.

9

"Who started this rumor?" he asked the tiger.

"It was the rhino," said the tiger.

10

"It was the rhino," said the tiger.

11

"It was the deer," said the rhino.

12

THE RIVER OF STARS

In this story from China, two lovers are separated until some magpies form a bridge with their wings to reunite them. This simple pop-up book explains both the origin of the Milky Way and the migration of birds.

Preparation:

Provide each child with a double-sided copy of pattern B on this page and a double-sided copy of page A. Children will need tape, scissors, and a stapler to make the book.

To Make the Mini-Book:

1. Cut this page along the midline. Place the side with pattern B on the desk so that the image faces up. This will be the "bridge of magpies" in the book.
2. Fold along the dotted lines closest to the ends. Crease sharply, then unfold again.
3. Flip the pattern over and fold along the dotted line in the middle. Crease sharply, then unfold. Cut along the outside edges then set bridge aside.
4. Cut along the solid line on page A to make two panels. (Do not cut along the shorter lines marked C and D.)
5. Fold each panel in half on the dotted line.

21 ∿∿∿∿∿

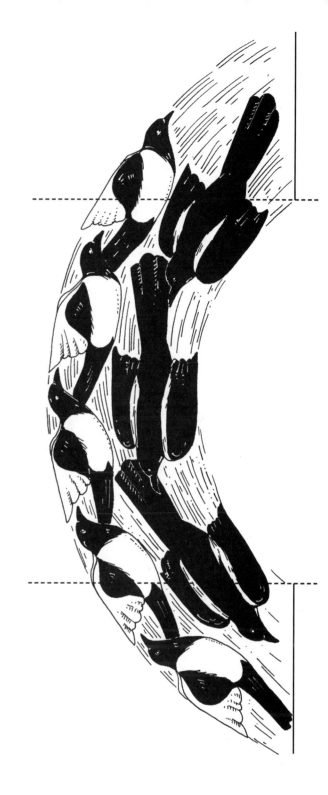

Pattern B
"Bridge of Magpies"

6. Nest the panels inside each other so that the pages of the book are in numerical order.

7. Close the book and position it so that the cover is face-up on the desk. Staple in the center to hold the pages together.

8. Open the book to pages 5-6. Take the bridge pattern and lay it across these pages. Place one end of the bridge on Line C on page 5 and the other on Line D on page 6, as shown in the diagram. Tape the bridge in place.

9. Fold the book closed, taking care that the bridge of magpies folds away from the spine.

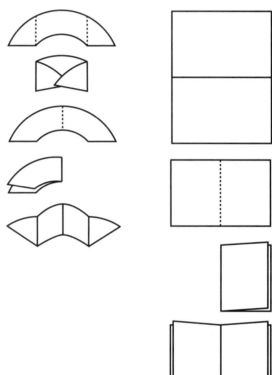

Tips for Reading:

When children read the book, the bridge of magpies will pop up to form a path between the herdsman and the sun goddess.

22

The River of Stars
A Folktale from China

Long ago, the sun god ruled over the stars and sky. His daughter was the goddess of weaving. On her loom, she spun the colors of the day. She wove the whispery pink of dawn and the glowing red of sunset.

1

"I am displeased," the sun god told them. The couple promised to return to their work.

But love proved stronger than promises. The loom stood idle. Oxen wandered the fields.

3

On earth, the magpies saw how unhappy the sun goddess and herdsman were. Then the birds thought of a way they could help the couple. Once a year the magpies meet above the Milky Way.

line C

6

One morning, the goddess met a herdsman leading his oxen to the water. The two fell in love and were soon married.

They were so happy that they forgot all about their work. No colors softened the harsh summer sun as it rose and set. No attention was paid to the oxen.

2

With their wings, they make a bridge across the river so that the sun goddess can spend a few, precious hours with her husband.

line D

7

The sun god grew angrier. "I will put an end to your foolishness!" he stormed.

He created a great river in the sky. The river ran so swift that no boat could cross it. It ran so wide that no bridge could span it. He called this river the Milky Way.

4

The sun god ordered, "My daughter shall live on one side of the river, her husband on the other."

Broken-hearted, the herdsman returned to the fields. Once again, the goddess sat at her loom.

5

Australia

THE FIRST SUNRISE

This Aboriginal myth explains how the magpies helped bring light to the world. Students will make a book in the same format as *Why the Sun and Moon Live in the Sky*.

Preparation:

Provide each student with a double-sided copy of page A. (One piece of paper, art and text on front and back.)

To Make the Mini-Book:

1. Place page A on the desk vertically.
2. Fold the top edge and bottom edge of the page toward the center by folding along the dotted line. Crease sharply.
3. Fold the top and the bottom toward the center again by folding along the dotted line. Crease sharply.
4. Fold the paper in half along the dotted line, folding the top down to meet the bottom so that the title of the book is face-up. Crease sharply.

Tips for Reading:

Unfold the top and bottom sections in reverse order to read the story. Be sure to unfold both the top and bottom of the page at the same time so that the illustrations correspond with the text. As children unfold the pages of the book, they will see the magpies raise the sky higher and higher until at last the sun bursts through. (Before reading, you may want to identify some of the animals in the story. Explain to children that magpies are a black-and-white bird related to jays, emus are ostrich-like birds, and goannas are large lizards.)

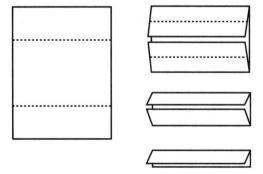

The magpies kept pushing and lifting, raising the sky higher and higher until suddenly. . .

THE FIRST SUNRISE

An Aboriginal Myth from Australia

Long ago, the sky wasn't up high like it is today. Instead, it hung close to the ground. It was black and thick and shut out all light. The animals couldn't even stand up. They had to crawl around in the darkness.

The magpies lived on the earth in great number. They grew tired of flying so close to the ground. So one day, the birds gathered some long, strong sticks. Then slowly and carefully, they began to lift the sky.

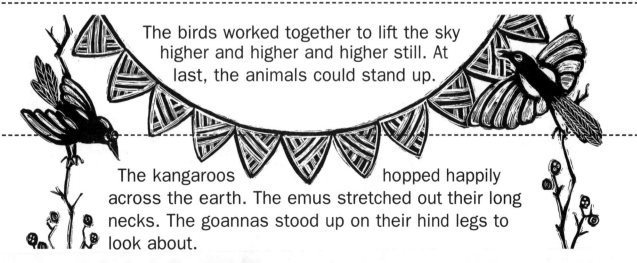

The birds worked together to lift the sky higher and higher and higher still. At last, the animals could stand up.

The kangaroos hopped happily across the earth. The emus stretched out their long necks. The goannas stood up on their hind legs to look about.

. . . the sky split open, and a great flood of light burst through and spilled over the earth. The animals looked up in amazement as the golden light spread across the sky. It was the first sunrise!

The magpies were so pleased with what they had done that they began to sing with joy.

To this day, the magpies greet the sun each morning with their happy warbling and remember how they lifted the sky and brought light to the world.

Eastern Europe

CZAR TROJAN'S EARS

This story from the former Yugoslavia tells how Czar Trojan comes to accept his unusual ears. Students will construct a book with a flap to lift and two tabs to pull. Assembling the book is a little tricky, but worth the extra time and effort.

Preparation:

Provide each child with a single-sided photocopy of the four tabs on page 31 and double-sided copies of pages A, B, and C. Children will need oak tag, glue, tape, scissors, and a stapler to make the book.

To Assemble the Pull-Tabs:

1. Cut out the half-page with tabs D, E, F, and G. Glue to oak tag. When dry, cut out the tabs.
2. Place page B horizontally on the desk.
3. Place Tab D on the page where indicated, with the writing side of tab facing down. About 1/4 inch of the tab should hang over the end of the page.
4. Place Tab E over Tab D, where indicated. Tape down the top and bottom of Tab E. Be careful not to tape down Tab D.
5. Check to be sure Tab D can slide easily back and forth through Tab E. Adjust

tape if necessary.
6. Flip the page over. Slide the strip into the slot so that only the end of tab D showing the musical note is visible.
7. Repeat steps 2-6 on Page C, using Tabs F and G.

To Make the Mini-Book:

1. Find the hat shape on page A. Cut along the solid lines of the hat to make an interior flap. (Do not cut along the dotted line.)
2. Place page A horizontally on the desk so that the "A" is at the top of the page. Fold the page in half along the horizontal dotted line, folding the top down to meet the bottom. Fold the page in half again along the vertical dotted line.
3. Repeat step 2 for pages B and C. Crease all folds well. When you have completed the folds, you should have three sections of the book.
4. Nest the sections of the book inside each other so that the pages are in numerical order.
5. Close the book and staple along the center spine to hold the pages together.

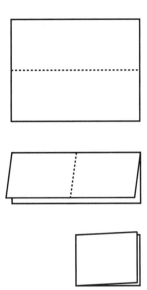

Tips for Reading:

As children read the book, invite them to fold the interior flap on page 1 to reveal Czar Trojan's secret. They can pull the tabs on pages 6 and 8 to "hear" the flute's song. After pulling tab out on each page, push back into its original position to prevent book from becoming unwieldy.

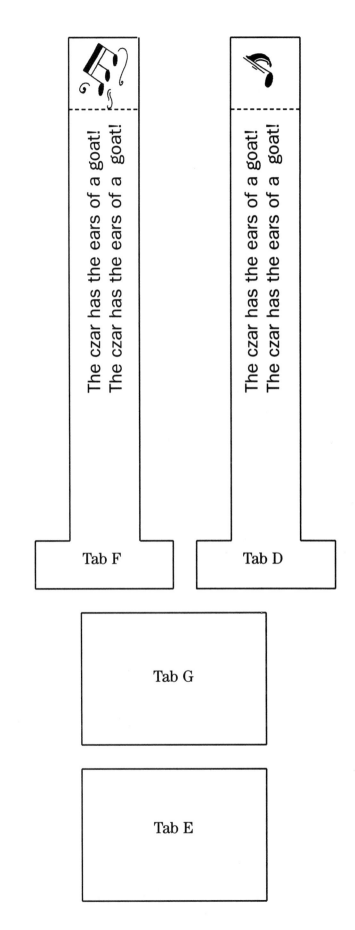

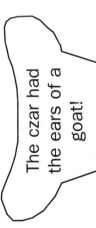

The czar had the ears of a goat!

Czar Trojan realized the barber was right. He would let the world see his unique ears. In gratitude, the czar gave his favorite hat to the barber. And whenever the czar heard the flute's song carried on the wind, he would wiggle his goat-like ears with pride.

CZAR TROJAN'S EARS

A FOLKTALE FROM EASTERN EUROPE

Long ago, there lived a czar named Trojan who always wore a hat. And under that hat he hid a secret. . .

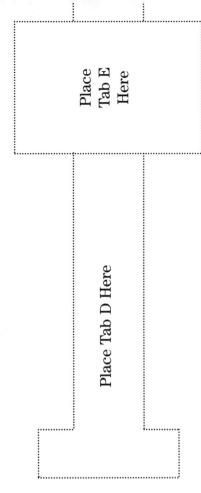

Place
Tab E
Here

Place Tab D Here

"How terrible!" said the czar sadly. "Now everyone knows my embarrassing secret."

"Sire, may I say something?" asked the barber. "Your ears are like no one else's. If I had your ears, I'd show them off."

The disbelieving czar ordered that the remaining tree branch be carved into a flute. And sure enough, when it was played the czar heard the flute sing his secret to the wind.

3

No one knew about Czar Trojan's ears except the barber who came to trim his hair. The czar had made the barber promise that he would never tell the secret of his goat-like ears to anyone.

The barber kept his promise, but it wasn't easy. He longed to tell someone about the czar's ears. Finally, the barber knew he could keep the secret no longer. So he dug a deep hole in the ground.

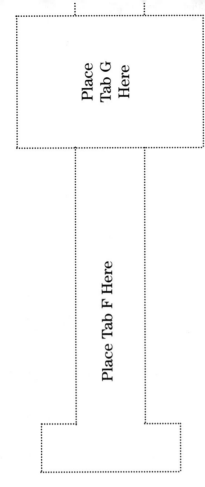

Place Tab F Here

Place
Tab G
Here

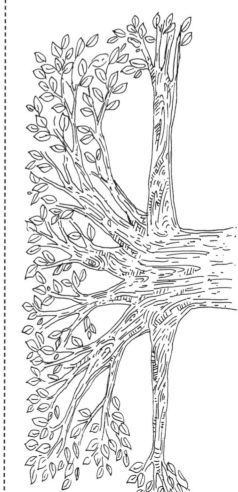

Then he stuck his head into the hole and shouted the secret as loud as he could:

"The czar has the ears of a goat! The czar has the ears of a goat! The czar has the ears of a goat!"

Much relieved, the barber covered his words with dirt and hurried away.

5

In time, a tree grew from the hole where the barber had shouted the secret. And from the tree grew two long, straight branches.

6

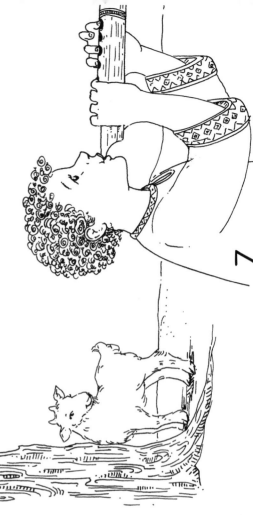

One day, a shepherd came upon the tree. He cut off a branch, carved it into a flute, and began to play. And what was the song that flute piped out?

7

The shepherd was quite surprised by the flute's song, and quickly spread the secret through the town. One morning, the czar himself heard some children whispering his secret to each other. He sent for the barber.

"Why have you told my secret?" the czar demanded.

"I give you my word, sire," the barber said, "I told your secret to no one but the earth." Then he explained about the hole, the tree, and the flute.

8

THE GREAT BIG ENORMOUS TURNIP

Children may be familiar with this well-known and well-loved cumulative story (adapted from Leo Tolstoy's classic retelling of the Russian folktale) about uprooting a stubborn turnip. For this project, they will construct a sliding strip book similar to *The Ostrich and the Crocodile.*

Preparation:

Provide each child with a single-sided copy of panel B and pull-tab C on this page and a double-sided copy of page A. Children will need tape and scissors to make the book.

To Make the Mini-Book:

1. Cut out panel B and from it cut pull-tab C.
2. Tape one end of pull-tab C to the right end of panel B. Set aside.
3. Cut out the box on the back of page A to make a window.
4. Turn over and hold horizontally with page A indicated at the top.
5. Fold the bottom edge of the page up to meet the top edge, folding along the dot-

(continued on back)

39

~~~~~~~~~~

Tape end of pull-tab C here.

. . . and POP! Up came the turnip. That night, there was turnip soup for everyone, with an extra large portion for the little bird.

Panel B

Pull-tab C

ted line. The text and illustrations should now be face-down.

6. Open the fold of page A and place panel B inside so that the text is face-down.
7. Tape along the top edges of the folded paper to hold panel B inside page A. Flip over.

(NOTE: When taping the edges closed, be careful not to tape down panel B. You should be able to slide panel B smoothly through folded page A.)

Tips for Reading:

Before reading, adjust sliding strip so that nothing is visible through the window. After reading the last block of text on the front of the book, pull the tab on the right to reveal the ending of the story and the turnip popping out of the ground. Advise children to only pull the sliding strip about half-way out, so that it doesn't slip out of its pocket.

THE GREAT BIG ENORMOUS TURNIP

A FOLKTALE FROM RUSSIA

Once an old man planted a turnip. "Grow big," he said to the turnip. "Grow strong." And the turnip did grow— VERY BIG and VERY STRONG.

When harvest time came, the old man grabbed hold of the great big enormous turnip's leaves and pulled and pulled. But the turnip would not come up.

The old man called his wife. The wife pulled the old man and the old man pulled the turnip. But

the turnip would not come up.

The old woman called the cat. The cat pulled the wife, the wife pulled the old man, and the old man pulled the

turnip. But the turnip would not come up.

The cat called a little bird. The bird pulled the cat, the cat pulled the wife and the wife pulled the old man and the old man pulled the turnip. . . .

Cut this out to make a "window."

Europe

THE TEENY TINY WOMAN

This familiar story from England is known as a "jump tale" because the ending, typically shouted as it's read, is meant to startle the reader. A series of cuts and folds on the accompanying pattern create a teeny tiny version of this spooky tale, with flaps to lift and peek under.

Preparation:

Provide each child with scissors, a stapler, and a double-sided photocopy of page A. Note that door flap cut lines are on the reverse of the illustrations.

To Make the Mini-Book:

1. Cut page A into four sections by cutting along the solid lines.
2. Cut the door flaps indicated by solid lines on the back of three of the mini-pages.
3. Fold along the dotted lines to make four sections that are the same size.

   (NOTE: Don't fold along the short, interior fold lines yet.)

4. Fold each section in half vertically and nest the sections inside one another so the pages are in numerical order.
5. Open the book so that the cover is face-up on the desk. Staple through the center fold line to complete the book. Make sure that the open end of the staple is in the center of the book for safety.

Tips for Reading:

Children can fold along the short dotted lines on pages 8, 15, and 16 to reveal surprises as they read the story.

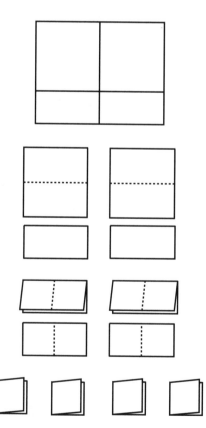

Once there was a teeny tiny woman who lived in a teeny tiny house in a teeny tiny town.

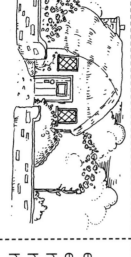

2

The Teeny Tiny Woman
A Folktale from England

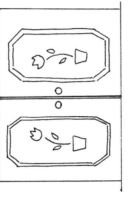

One evening, the teeny tiny woman went for a teeny tiny walk in the teeny tiny park near her teeny tiny house.

3

And even though she was even a teeny tiny bit more frightened, the teeny tiny woman poked her teeny tiny head from under her teeny tiny blanket and said in her loudest teeny tiny voice:

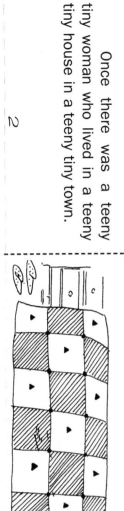

16

Just as she was falling back to sleep, the teeny tiny woman heard the teeny tiny voice come again a teeny tiny bit louder:

Give me back my bone!

14

So the teeny tiny woman put the teeny tiny bone into her teeny tiny cupboard.

Once home, the teeny tiny woman began to feel a teeny tiny bit tired. "I think I will take a teeny tiny nap," she said.

7

"I could boil this teeny tiny bone and make a teeny tiny pot of soup for my supper," said the teeny tiny woman.

5

Then she climbed into her teeny tiny bed and closed her teeny tiny eyes.

9

She had just fallen asleep when she was awakened by a teeny tiny voice coming from the teeny tiny cupboard:

Give me back my bone!

10

Then she heard the teeny tiny voice again, this time a teeny tiny bit louder:

Give me back my bone!

12

And as the teeny tiny woman walked along the teeny tiny path in the teeny tiny park she found a teeny tiny bone.

4

This made the teeny tiny woman a teeny tiny bit more afraid, so she pulled the teeny tiny blanket a teeny tiny bit higher over her teeny tiny head.

13

The end.

TAKE IT!

So she picked up the teeny tiny bone, put it in her teeny tiny pocket, and walked back to her teeny tiny house.

6

This made the teeny tiny woman a teeny tiny bit scared, so she pulled the teeny tiny blanket over her teeny tiny head.

11

THE WEE BANNOCK

Countries all around the world tell different versions of this cumulative story about a baked item on the run from a succession of hungry people and animals. This version from Scotland features a bannock, which is a small oaten cake. (Your class may notice the story's similarity to the popular tale "The Gingerbread Man.") Children will construct a book with a "wee bannock" that actually turns as it rolls away from its pursuers.

Preparation:

Provide each child with a single-sided copy of the three bannock patterns on page 48 and a double-sided photocopy of pages A and B. Children will need scissors, glue, oak tag, brass paper fasteners, and a stapler to complete the book.

To Assemble the Bannocks:

1. Cut out the three bannocks at the bottom of the next page.
2. Trace the bannock shapes onto oak tag and cut out the cardboard circles.
3. Glue a bannock shape onto each circle.
4. Stick a brass paper fastener through the dot at the center of each bannock.

   (Note: You may want to poke a hole in the cardboard with a pencil or pen point first, to make it easier to insert the paper fastener.)

To Attach the Bannocks to the Mini-Book:

1. Place pages A and B on the desk.
2. Find the mini-book pages numbered 3, 5, and 7. Poke a paper fastener (still attached to a bannock) through each of the dots in the centers of the bannock illustrations.
3. Turn the page over and open the fasteners to hold the bannocks in place on the paper.

   (NOTE: Don't make the fasteners grip the paper too tightly; there should be some play so that the bannocks can turn easily.)

To Make the Mini-Book:

1. Find mini-book page 8 on the back of page A. Cut along the solid line to make an interior flap that will be lifted as you read the story.
2. Place page A vertically on the desk, with the A at the top of the paper.
3. Fold page A in half along the dotted lines, folding the top of the page down to

meet the bottom.

4. Fold in half again along the dotted line.

5. Repeat steps 2-4 for page B. You will have two folded sections.

6. Nest the two sections inside each other so that the pages of the book are in numerical order.

7. Place the book on the desk so that the cover faces up. Staple along the center spine. Be careful not to staple the flap on top of the last page.

Tips for Reading:

As you read the book, turn the bannocks clockwise to mimic their rolling motion. On page 8, fold the flap down along the dotted line to reveal the bannock's fate.

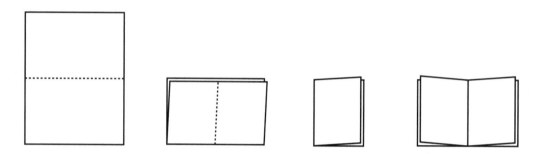

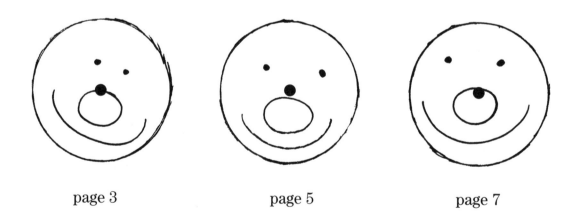

page 3   page 5   page 7

Before long, the bannock came upon a fox, and called,
"I've run from the woman,
I've run from the man
I've run from the sheep
And her little lamb
I've run from the goat, nanny-nan-nan
And I can run from you, too,
I can! I can!"

But by now the little cake was fair puggled.* And the fox, who could run very fast, caught the wee bannock and ate it up.

tired

8

The Wee Bannock

a Folktale from Scotland

Once a woman made a bannock for her husband's breakfast. A wee bit of a cake, it was, too. Ah, but the smell of it made her husband's mouth water!

But as the woman lifted the bannock from the pan, it fell to the floor and began to roll.

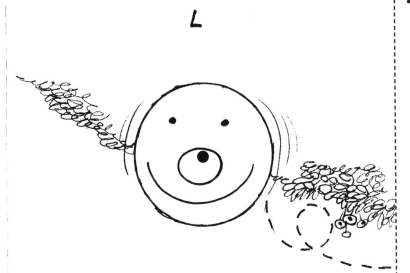

7

The nanny goat ran after the wee bannock, but it rolled away too fast and she couldn't catch it.

"Oh, ye're nippin's! ye're nippins!" cried the bannock. And, sad but true, those were the last words the wee bannock ever spoke.

Next, the wee bannock came upon a nanny goat. As it rolled by, the bannock called,

"I've run from the woman,
I've run from the man,
I've run from the sheep,
and her little lamb.
And I can run from you, too,
I can! I can!"

6

The wee bannock rolled out the door, through the gate, and down the hill. The man and woman chased after it, but the wee bannock rolled away too fast and they couldn't catch it.

3

4

Soon the wee bannock came to a meadow where a sheep and her lamb were grazing. As it rolled by the bannock called,

"I've run from the woman,
I've run from the man
And I can run from you, too,
I can! I can!"

5

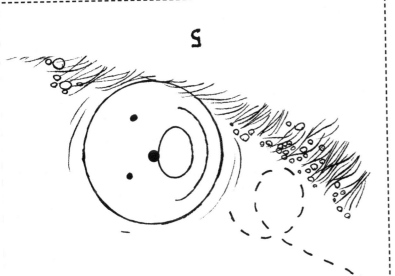

And so the sheep and her little lamb began to chase after the cake. But the bannock rolled away too fast, and they couldn't catch it.

TOADS AND DIAMONDS

In this French fairy tale made classic by Charles Perrault, a good sister and an evil sister get their just rewards for their respective behavior. Children will create a book with two pull-tabs, similar to *Czar Trojan's Ears*.

Preparation:

Provide each child with a single-sided photocopy of the tab patterns on page 54 and double-sided copies of pages A and B. Children will need scissors, oak tag, glue, tape, and a stapler to make the book.

To Assemble the Pull-Tabs:

1. Glue the half-page with tabs C, D, E, and F onto oak tag. Cut out the tabs.
2. Place page B on the desk so that it is positioned horizontally.
3. Place Tab C on the page where indicated, with the picture side of tab facing down. About 1/4 inch of the tab should hang over the end of the page.
4. Place Tab D over Tab C, where indicated. Tape down the top and bottom of Tab D. Be careful not to tape down Tab C.
5. Check to be sure Tab C can slide easily back and forth through Tab D. Adjust tape if necessary.

6. Repeat steps 2 through 5 using tabs E and F, placing tabs where indicated.
7. Flip the page over. Check to be sure the strips are positioned in the slots so that only the ends of the tab are visible.

To Make the Mini-Book:

1. Place page A horizontally on the desk so that the letter A is at the top of the page. Cut the page in half along the solid line.
2. Fold each panel in half along the dotted line.
3. Position page B horizontally on the desk so that the letter B is at the top of the page. Fold along the dotted line, folding the top down to meet the bottom.
4. Fold the page in half again along the dotted line.
5. You should now have three sections of the book. Nest the three sections inside of each other so that the pages of the book are in numerical order.
6. Open the book and place it face-down on the desk so that the cover faces up. Staple through the center spine to complete the book. Make sure that the open end of the staple is in the center of the book for safety.

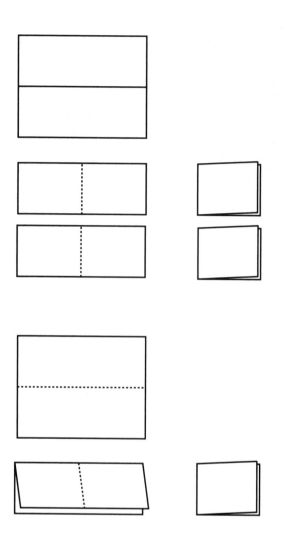

Tips for Reading:

As you read the book, pull the tabs on pages 5 and 8 to see what enchantment befalls each sister. After pulling tab out on each page, push back into its original position to prevent book from becoming unwieldy.

54

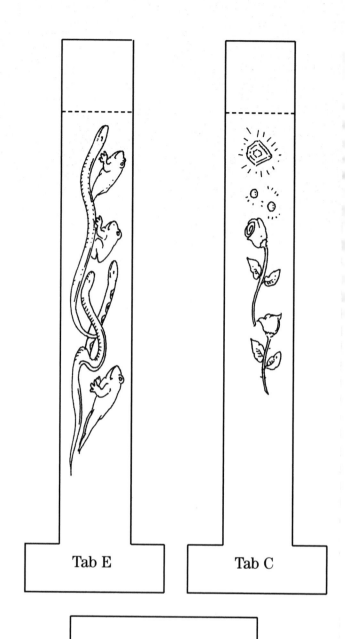

Tab E

Tab C

Tab F

Tab D

Toads and Diamonds
A Folktale from France

Once upon a time, there lived a woman who had two daughters. Now the younger daughter was generous and kind-hearted, but the older one was greedy and mean.

One day, the young girl was fetching water from the fountain when a poor old woman came by and begged for a drink. "Drink as much as you like," said the girl kindly, pouring water into a tin cup for the woman.

3

From then on, the older daughter clasped her hand over her mouth every time she got the urge to talk. And never again did the girl order her younger sister around or say an unkind word to her.

The older girl treated the younger one cruelly. She made her sister do all the chores while she ordered her about and complained of how poorly she did them.

2

"Thank you, child. I wish to repay your kindness with a gift," said the woman. "With every word you speak, out of your mouth will come a flower or a jewel."

4

11

"Mercy!" cried her mother. As her oldest daughter shrieked in horror, more toads and snakes dropped from her tongue. "Don't speak! It's too terrible!" said her mother.

9

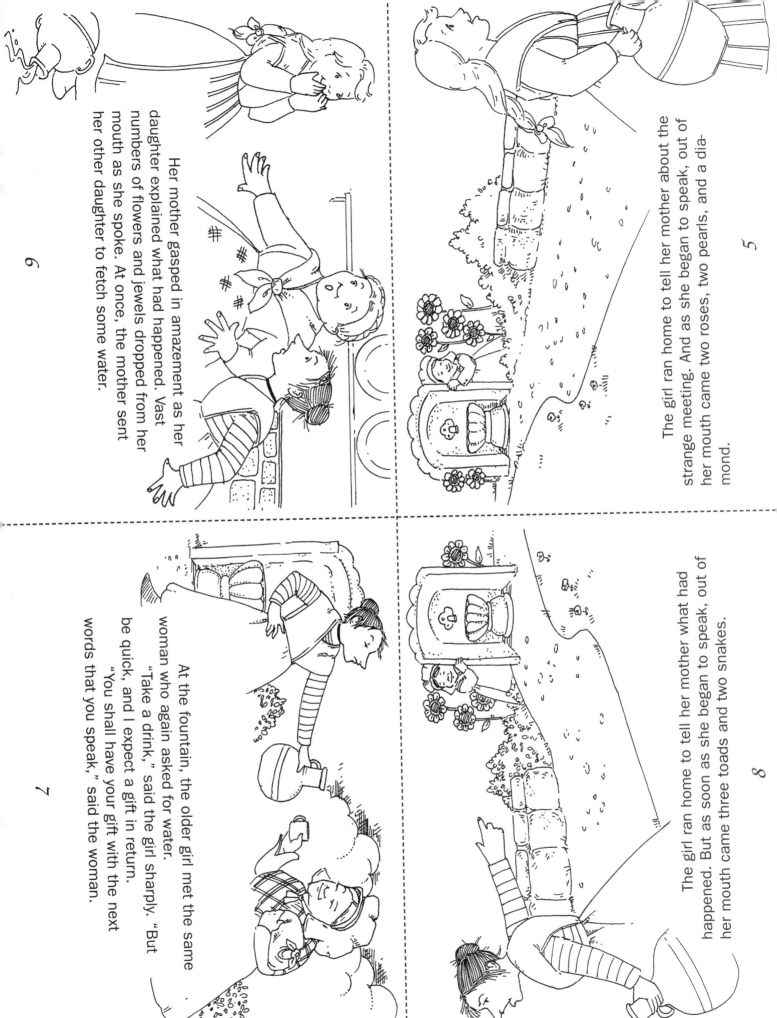

6

Her mother gasped in amazement as her daughter explained what had happened. Vast numbers of flowers and jewels dropped from her mouth as she spoke. At once, the mother sent her other daughter to fetch some water.

5

The girl ran home to tell her mother about the strange meeting. And as she began to speak, out of her mouth came two roses, two pearls, and a diamond.

7

At the fountain, the older girl met the same woman who again asked for water.

"Take a drink," said the girl sharply. "But be quick, and I expect a gift in return."

"You shall have your gift with the next words that you speak," said the woman.

8

The girl ran home to tell her mother what had happened. But as soon as she began to speak, out of her mouth came three toads and two snakes.

Place
Tab D
Here

Place Tab C Here

Place Tab E Here

Place
Tab F
Here

THE THREE BILLYGOATS GRUFF

Children will make a lift-the-flap book with a few hidden surprises for this retelling of the well-known and well-loved folktale from Norway.

Preparation:

Provide each child with a double-sided photocopy of pages A, B, C, and D. Children will need scissors and a stapler to make the book.

To Make to Mini-Book:

1. Cut along all solid lines on all pages to make interior flaps.
2. Position page A vertically on the desk. Fold in half along the dotted line, folding the bottom of the page up to meet the top.
3. Fold page in half again along the long vertical dotted line. Crease all folds sharply.

   (NOTE: Do not fold along the shortest dotted lines yet. Students will fold these back as they read the book to reveal surprises.)

4. Repeat steps 2 and 3 for pages B, C, and D. You should have four sections of the book.
5. Nest the four sections inside one another so that the pages are in numerical order.
6. Tape the tops of pages 11 and 12 together back-to-back with clear tape, making sure not to tape the bottom flap closed.
7. Open the book so that the cover is face-up on the desk. Staple through the center fold line to complete the book. Make sure that the open end of the staple is in the center of the book for safety.

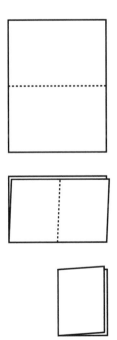

Tips for Reading:

As children read the book, have them fold along the dotted lines to lift the flaps and reveal the troll hiding on pages 2, 4, 6, 8, and 13. On page 11, they can fold along the dotted line to lift the flap and see how the third billygoat Gruff puts an end to their troubles with the troll!

THE THREE BILLYGOATS GRUFF

A FOLKTALE FROM NORWAY

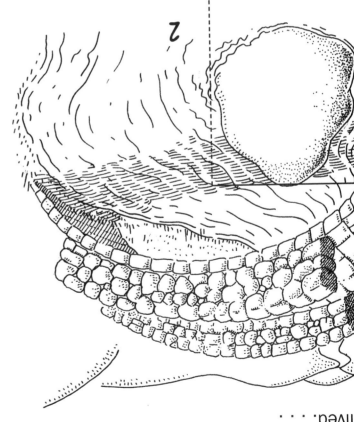

Once there were three billygoats whose name was Gruff. One day, the first billygoat decided to go to the hillside to make himself fat.

15

This tale's told out.

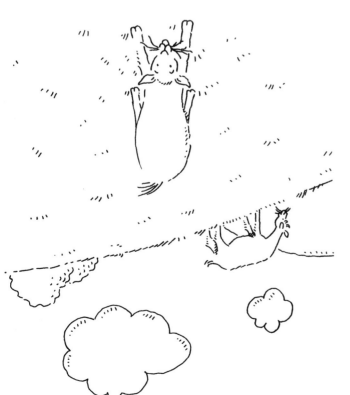

2

But to get to the hillside, the billygoat had to first cross a bridge. And under that bridge, behind a huge rock, there lived . . .

. . . a horrible, terrible troll.

Snip, snap, snout.

14

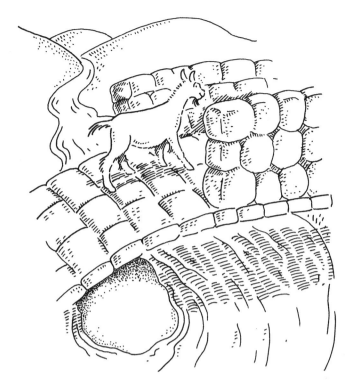

The first billygoat began to cross the bridge, trip trap, trip trap, trip trap.

3

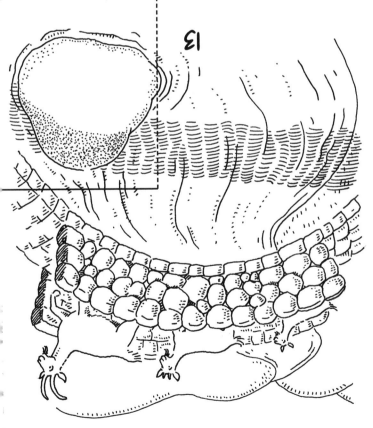

And when they crossed back over the bridge to return home, guess what they heard from below?

13

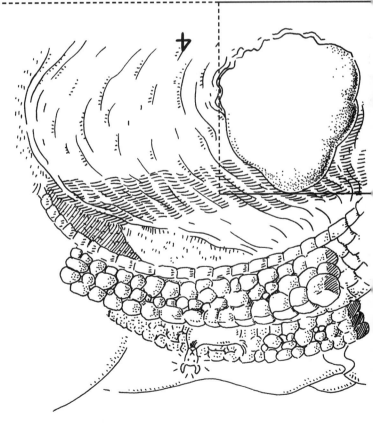

Suddenly, he heard a loud, angry voice from below:

4

Nothing. For the horrible, terrible troll had found a new bridge to live under, and he never bothered the three billy-goats Gruff again.

"Who dares to cross my bridge? I'm going to gobble you up!"

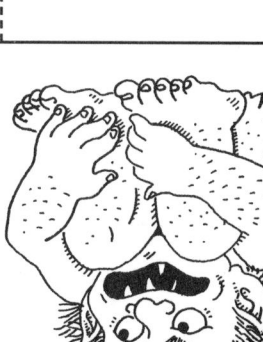

And so the third billygoat Gruff joined his brothers on the hillside, and they all ate and ate until they couldn't eat any more.

12

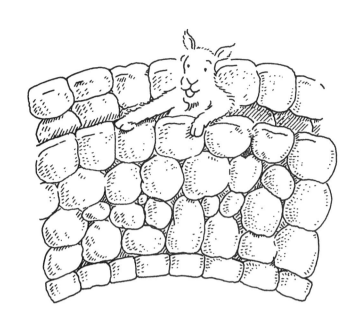

"Oh, no-don't eat me," said the first billygoat Gruff. "Wait a bit for my brother. He's much bigger than I, and will fill you up." And so the troll let him pass.

5

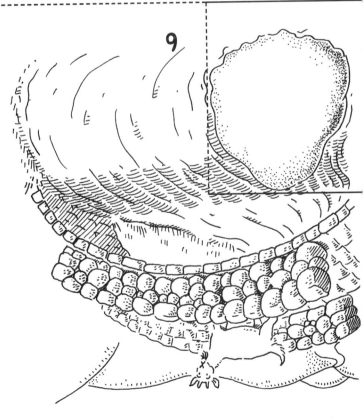

9

Soon, the second billygoat Gruff came over the bridge, TRIP TRAP, TRIP TRAP, TRIP TRAP. Suddenly, he heard a voice from below:

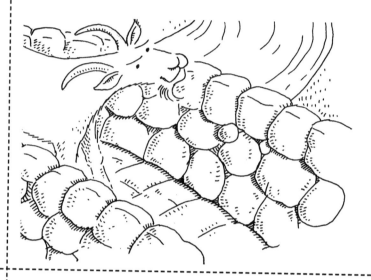

"Who dares
to cross
my bridge?
I'm going
to gobble
you up!"

So out jumped the troll to gobble up the third billygoat Gruff. But before he could get even a nibble, the big billygoat butted him so hard and threw him so high that he flew up into the sky and far out into the water.

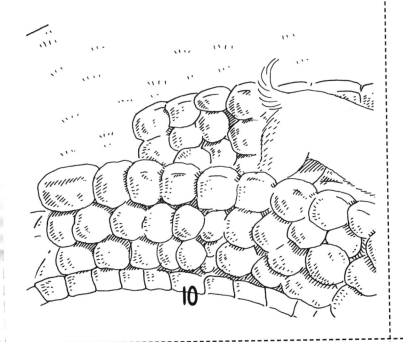

10

"Don't eat me!" said the second billy-goat Gruff. "Wait for my brother, for he is much bigger than I, and he will fill you up." And so the troll let him pass.

7

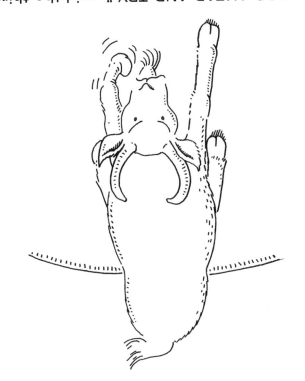

9

"GO AHEAD AND TRY," said the third and biggest billygoat Gruff, who wasn't the least bit afraid of the terrible, horrible troll.

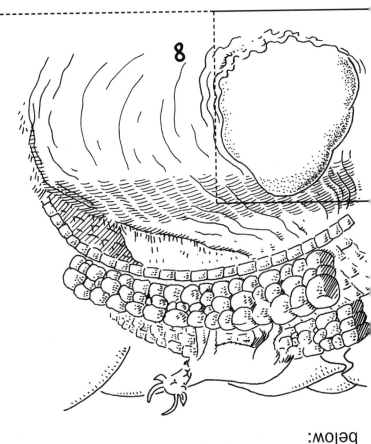

8

Finally, the third and biggest billygoat Gruff came along, TRIP TRAP TRIP TRAP TRIP TRAP. And he, too, heard a voice from below:

"Who dares
to cross
my bridge?
I'm going
to gobble
you up!"

North America

THE FIRST BUTTERFLIES

This Native American legend recounts how the first butterflies came to be. Children will make a pop-up book in which a folded chain of butterflies magically emerges as the story is read.

Preparation:

Provide children with double-sided photocopies of pages A and B. Children will need scissors, tape or glue, crayons, and a stapler to make the book.

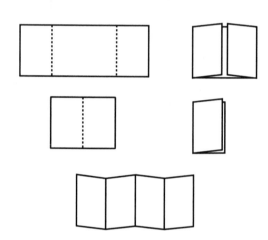

To Make the Butterfly Chain:

1. Cut out panel C on page A. Position so that the side with the butterfly pattern is face-up on the desk.
2. You are going to make a series of accordion-like folds. Begin by folding the two ends up toward the center along the dotted lines. Flip the strip over and fold in half.
3. Open the folds to reveal the chain of butterflies. Cut close around the four butterflies being careful to keep them all attached at the wings. Color all the butterflies bright colors. Set aside.

To Make the Mini-Book:

1. Place page B horizontally on the desk, so that the letter B is at the bottom of the paper. Cut along the solid line to make two panels.
2. Fold each panel in half along the dotted line.
3. Place the bottom section of page A horizontally on the desk. Fold the panel in half along the dotted line.
4. You should now have three panels. Nest the panels inside of each other so that the pages of the book are in numerical order.

5. Open the book so that the cover is face-up on the desk. Staple through the center fold line to complete the book. Make sure that the open end of the staple is in the center of the book for safety.

6. Open the book to pages 6-7. Glue or tape one end of the butterfly chain in position over line D on page 6. Glue or tape the other end of the butterfly chain in position over line E on page 7.

7. Fold the book closed, taking care that the butterflies fold away from the spine of the book.

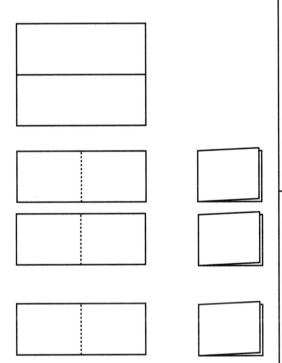

Tips for Reading:

When you turn to pages 6-7 of the book, the chain of butterflies should pop up and out of the book.

71 ~~~~~~~~~

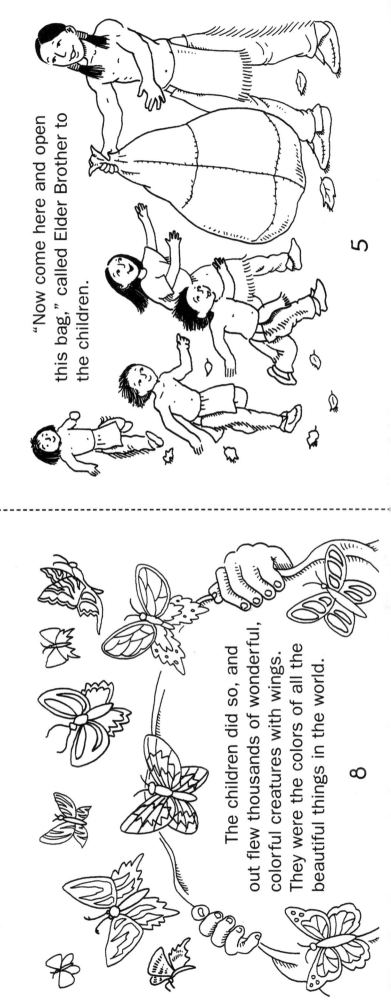

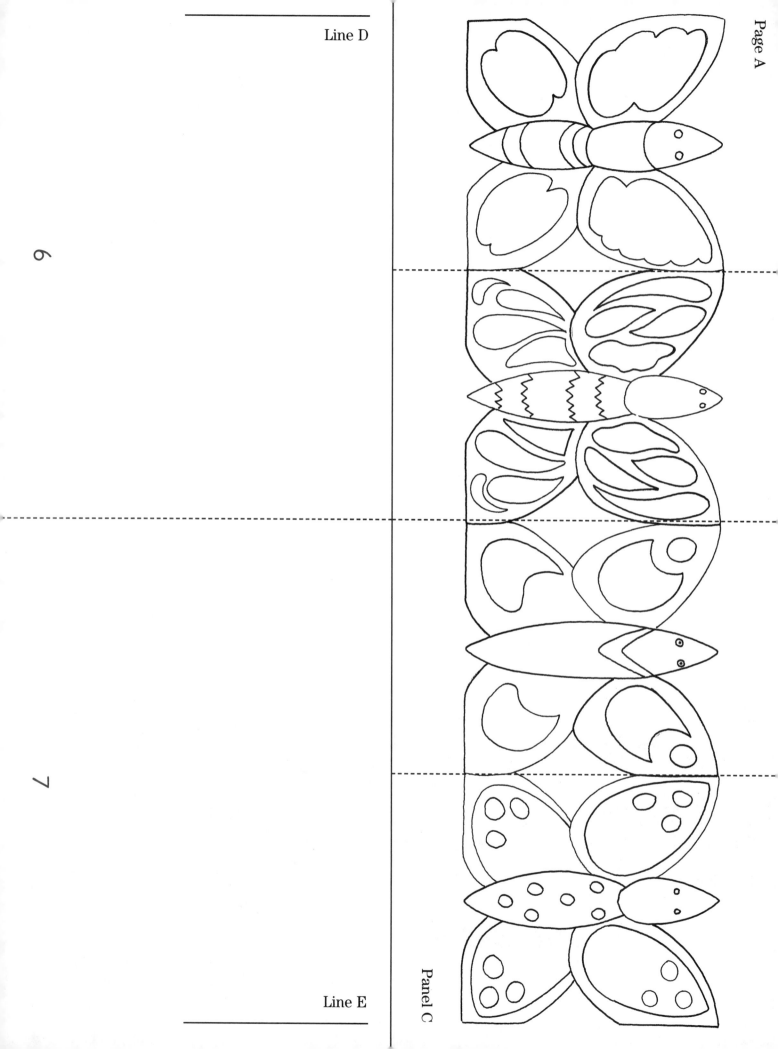

Line D

6

7

Line E

Panel C

The First Butterflies

A Native American Legend

Adapted from a Retelling
by Joseph Bruchac

Long ago, when the world was very new, Elder Brother walked around Earth to enjoy the beauty of it. He watched the young children. Everywhere on Earth, they were playing.

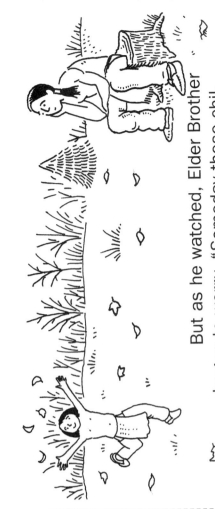

But as he watched, Elder Brother began to worry. "Someday these children may be sad," he thought. "They may get sick or be hungry. They may get cold in the snow, or be blown about by harsh winds."

3

"These are new creatures called butterflies," said Elder Brother. "I made them for you. If times come when you are sad, the sight of butterflies may cheer you up."

10

"How happy the children are!" thought Elder Brother. "They love the soft rain, the green of the grass. They love the bright leaves that fall from the trees and fly through the breeze."

2

Then Elder Brother had an idea that made him smile again. He got a big bag and filled it with flowers and red and yellow leaves. He put in some blue feathers of the jaybird, some blades of green grass, some golden corn. He added a bit of sunshine.

4

And to this day, it is so. The butterflies dance and flutter and fly and make children happy.

11

"What are they? What are they?" cried the children. They laughed and clapped with joy as the creatures flew about their heads.

9

ANTONIO'S LUCKY DAY

In this project, children construct a book with a turning wheel that reveals a dream sequence of lucky things that might happen if only young Antonio can catch and sell a fat rabbit.

Preparation:

Provide each child with a single-sided photocopy of the two wheel patterns on the back of this page and double-sided photocopies of pages A and B. Children will need oak tag, glue, tape, scissors, brass paper fasteners, a pen, and a stapler to make the book.

To Make the Turning Wheel:

1. Cut out wheel C and wheel D.
2. Place one of the wheels on a piece of oak tag, trace it, and cut out the circle.
3. Paste wheels C and D to either side of the oaktag circle.
4. Make a small hole in the center of the wheel by poking it with the point of a pen. Set aside.

To Make the Mini-Book:

1. Cut along the solid lines on page A to make two "windows".
2. Flip the page and poke a brass paper fastener through the dot under the window on mini-book page 3.
3. Flip the page over and fasten wheel D facing up. Open the ends of the fastener.
4. Fold the page in half along the dotted line. Tape pages 3 and 4 of the book together along the top, bottom, and right-hand side, to contain wheel. Put page, with wheels attached, aside.

   (NOTE: Do not tape the part of the page where the wheel sticks out. The wheel must turn smoothly.)

5. Place page B on the desk and fold along the dotted line, and nest taped pages 3-4 inside folded page B, with the pages of the mini-book in numerical order.
6. Close the book so that the cover is face-up on the desk. Staple along the center fold line to complete the book.

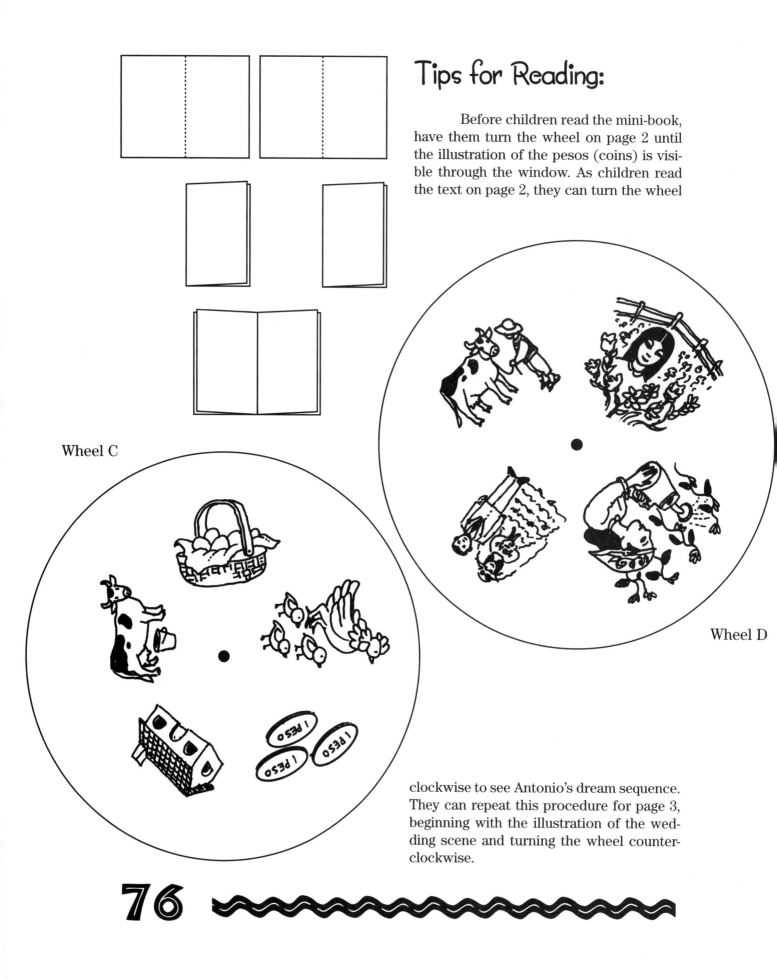

Tips for Reading:

Before children read the mini-book, have them turn the wheel on page 2 until the illustration of the pesos (coins) is visible through the window. As children read the text on page 2, they can turn the wheel

Wheel C

Wheel D

clockwise to see Antonio's dream sequence. They can repeat this procedure for page 3, beginning with the illustration of the wedding scene and turning the wheel counterclockwise.

Antonio's Lucky Day

A Folktale from Mexico

Retold by Joe Hayes

Antonio was a poor farmer's son. He had no money. He had no chickens. He had no cows. But he held his head high, and he walked with a happy step.

Antonio laughed at his own bad luck. "At least I was rich for a minute," he said. "Maybe tomorrow will be my lucky day." Then, with a kick in his step and a dream in his eye, Antonio walked toward home.

6

And he told anyone who would listen that someday he would be rich. "*Quien sabe?* Who knows?" he would say. "It might be today. This feels like my lucky day."

One day, Antonio was out walking when a rabbit hopped out of a thicket.

If I can catch that rabbit I can sell it at the market, Antonio thought.

2

At the sound of Antonio's voice, the rabbit leaped high into the air. Then it hopped back into the thicket, taking all of Antonio's plans with it.

5

Antonio smiled to think of the jingle of pesos in his pocket. Then I'll buy a hen, he thought. Soon she'll hatch out babies. I'll sell some eggs each day. Before long, I'll buy a cow. I'll sell the milk at the market, too, and use the money to build a house.

Then I'll ask Isabela to marry me, Antonio thought. We'll settle down to a happy life. I'll take care of the animals while Isabela tends the chile patch. But what's this I see? She's watering the chiles! She shouldn't do that now that they are ripening. They won't turn out good and hot. Antonio waved his arms and shouted, "No, Isabela! Stop!"

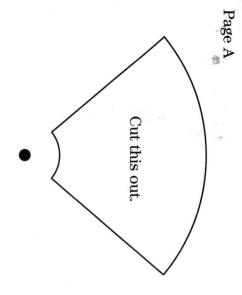

Cut this out.

DISCARD

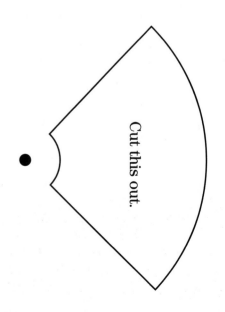

Cut this out.